MISSONI

MISSONI

Edited by Samuele Mazza
Text by Mariuccia Casadio

Gingko PRESS

On the cover
Photograph by Mario Testino

Opening pages
Terry-knit beach co-ordinates
(photograph by M. Testino)

Man's fabric suit and space-dyed knitted
shirt (photograph by M. Testino)

Beach sandals made from a mixture
of materials (photograph by G. Mocafico)

Man's lightweight knitted shirt
(photograph by M. Testino)

Translated from the Italian by Ruth Taylor

First published in Italy:
© 1997 by Leonardo Arte s.r.l., Milano, Elemond Editori Associati
All rights reserved

Published in the United States of America by Gingko Press Inc.
5768 Paradise Drive, Suite J - Corte Madera, CA 94925
Tel: (415) 924-9615 - Fax: (415) 924-9608 - email: gingko@linex.com

ISBN 3-927258-47-4

Printed in Italy

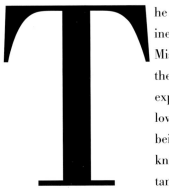

The 'fashion' product and the lifestyle of its creator are inextricably linked. Indeed, in the case of the Missonis, the predominating spirit is one that reflects the couple's everyday reality, that is to say, it is an expression of great stylistic consistency, of loyalty and love for one material, wool, which has led to their being consecrated world leaders in the field of knitwear. The Missonis occupy a particularly important place in the history of Italian fashion. Their products are ideally conceived to bear the Missoni label, in the sense that they are so original that they are impossible to imitate. Indeed, anyone who has attempted to mix or space-dye yarns has merely obtained a copy, some kind of by-product. Another characteristic of the Missonis is that they are the only official 'married' couple in international fashion; untainted by the usual rivalry between couples, Ottavio and Rosita serve as an example twice over. On a personal level, they have produced a wonderful family to which they have managed to convey their passion for this profession, and in addition, through the stubbornness and hard work typical of the successful, they have achieved their ultimate dream in style.

We wish them even greater success in the future and are grateful to them for having given us, through their products, the joy and enthusiasm typical of two such confirmed optimists.

Samuele Mazza

The nineties have marked the beginning of a particularly happy chapter in the story of Tai and Rosita Missoni, two of the best-known and best-loved protagonists of Italian *prêt-à-porter*. They are known not only for their stylistic variation, increasingly modern and in tune with current trends in fashion, but also for the advances they have made in technological and manufacturing processes. The success of their latest collections and the internationally recognized talents of their children, Angela, Luca and Vittorio, who have been partially responsible for a 'relaunching' of the company through fresh creativity and new, highly sophisticated machinery, have resulted in a wave of recent interest. This comes from a younger public, from the specialist European and American press and, lastly, from the friends and supporters of a trademark that could be described as one of the most consistently prolific and enduring on the international fashion scene.

So, M for Missoni. But also for museum exhibitions. Museumization. Missonologia! The latter stands for the association between the finished products, made in wools, silks, cottons, linens and viscose with the help of computerized looms, and the careful blend of colour and design; through unfailingly original tonalities, Missoni symbolizes the ultimate in luxury and aesthetic delight.

This environment is conducive to creating a special relationship with art and an entirely new approach to knitwear, introducing the latter to the fashion arena but not forsaking its practical function. In short, it can by now be defined as a philosophy or an aesthetic vision applied to contemporary lifestyle. In 1994, with 'Missonologia', the retrospective exhibition accompanied by a catalogue published by Electa, the Florentine fair Pitti Immagine paid homage to Rosita and Ottavio Missoni's vision of fashion, celebrating, as the opening dedication states, the fortieth anniversary of an 'inimitable and extraordinary career'. In a series of essays written by Anna Piaggi, Enzo Biagi, Emilio Tadini and Carlo Arturo Quintavalle, together with a selection of articles and reviews, and through the use of a wealth of

Seventies-inspired zigzag suit

images, the catalogue examines the Missonis' remarkable and precursory achievements in the history of knitwear. Quintavalle talks of 'a new way of weaving wool, of programming computers to produce new designs'; he describes their success as going 'against the current... different from all the others... an incomparable act on the cutting edge.'

Today, in response to the changing demands of fashion consumers, the space-dyed and zigzag motifs are once again a must. The Missonis are relaunching them with incredible creative energy, but without self-reference or repetition. At Rosita's side, Angela now plays a part in creating the new Missoni womenswear collections, as well as having established a new line bearing her own name; Luca, who has become art director, carries out a broad range of creative roles, from investigating yarns to keeping abreast of the latest in technology, from developing abstract and figurative motifs on computer to organizing fashion shows and exhibitions; Vittorio, the marketing manager, has taken on the diplomatic role of 'frontman', attentive to the demands of a well-established clientele as well as to those of new followers.

'We work in a company which is unique', explains Vittorio, the eldest, 'creating a product which, in its turn, is unique. We are talking about extreme exclusivity, both with regard to the company's image and to the creative and technical typology of our products. We invent fashion, but also knitwear. Maintaining the powerful and instantly recognizable image that we have created for Missoni, when there is no real competition on the market, calls for constant attention and updating. From a commercial point of view, too, everything is based on a delicate balancing act, aimed at never inflating the value of our product.'

Uniqueness has been a feature of this fashion venture right from the start. The Missonis' story has in fact developed along a logical path, characterized by a relentlessly eclectic approach and a multiplicity of cultural interests, ranging from art to ethnic cultures, which were already apparent at the very outset of the creative partnership of the two founders, Ottavio and Rosita.

Born respectively in Dalmatia and in a small town on the banks of the Ticino, in the province of Varese, the two laid the foundations for the opening of their first

The entire Missoni family
(photograph by O. Toscani)

workshop in 1953, in the basement of 12, Via Vespucci, Gallarate, the house where they settled immediately after their marriage. The workshop marked the initial fulcrum, the first tangible sign, of an indisputably happy and fruitful union. From then onwards, the couple's fortunes were to become entwined with the rediscovery of machinery which had traditionally been employed in the the manufacture of, for example, shawls, but had never been used to create garments such as jackets and overcoats, let alone to design entire *prêt-à-porter* collections. The first collection, christened 'Milano-Simpathy' and produced in 1958 for La Rinascente department stores, led to their meeting Anna Piaggi, with whom they still maintain an important professional, and close personal, relationship. It was Piaggi who introduced the Missonis' earliest ideas to the pages of the magazine *Arianna*, thus establishing a popularity that was destined to increase and spread in following years. The genius behind avant-garde, as well as aesthetically remarkable, creations, the Missonis have transformed knitwear into a symbol of our time – one of Italian fashion's most significant and recognized international achievements.

Speaking of his childhood and adolescence, Luca recalls, 'As far back as I can remember, we always had fun playing in the factory. In my case, machines, mechanisms and anything to do with technology – though less the actual machines, and more what they can do – have always aroused my curiosity. I love discovering their potential, looking beyond the purpose for which a particular mechanism was invented. And the factory has always given me the opportunity to explore and develop ideas. This is an attitude that I have had since I was a child when I used to spend whole afternoons playing at the factory. Then we moved to Sumirago when I was sixteen and I realized that my real passion lay in just standing there and seeing what those machines could create. Watching them, whole evenings would go by

Left, reels of yarn; right, loom

Following pages:
Left, colour variations of the yarn used in the coat on the right; right, tweed-effect knitted coat inspired by autumn colours (photograph by D. Malerbi)

20

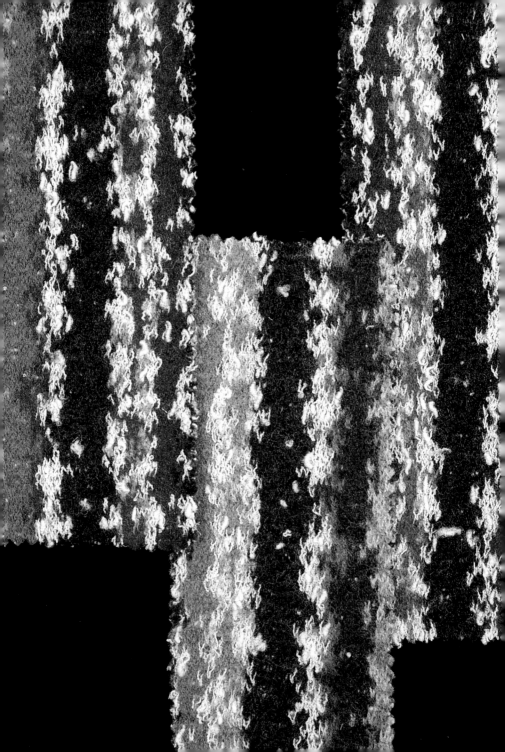

without my even noticing.... You stand there, you make samples, you try out your own ideas.... And so, several years later, once I'd finished secondary school and enrolled at university, I realized that I was spending most of my time designing fabrics, rather than studying for my exams. This went on until, once I'd finished my national service, I decided to join the factory – making the decision which, subconsciously, I had made long before. My interests and my responsibilities in the company still include design and its uses. I like applying art to the technology available and vice versa.'

Angela Missoni, too, is now an invaluable member of the team. In addition to launching her own collection, acclaimed by the international press over the last few seasons, Angela complements her mother Rosita's sensitivity and design talents. 'I started to work in the business when I was very young', she recalls, 'about eighteen or twenty years old. Having spent years immersed in the stimulating aura of Missoni's success in the fashion world, I grew close to my mother working as an assistant.... Then, when I started, I was surprised to sense an atmosphere of conservatism and I noticed that my mother, too, had far less enthusiasm than in the past. Unfortunately, when you have a strong, clearly defined and recognizable identity, like Missoni, clients always ask you for the same things. They cling stubbornly to the idea that there is only one type of jacket, or sweater, or reversible overcoat.... In the meantime, I had three children and every time I returned to the company I always had the same reaction, "No, I want to do something else." So I went ahead with other projects, like a playgroup in Varese, for example.... My relationship with my mother is founded on mutual understanding. She tried to leave me space, but I am someone who doesn't know how to accept it unless I am really sure of how to use it. So I decided to leave the business. At that point, my father said, "You don't have to work so closely with your mother. There are plenty of other things you can do in the company." Initially I worked on the company's licensed products – handbags, glasses, perfumes – trying to maintain a certain distance from the industrial side. Then, five years ago, there was another opportunity – the chance to create a collection under my own name. My mother was wholeheartedly in favour, particularly because she found it impossible to design clothes in a single colour. The expectations of clients, accustomed to

associating Missoni with colour and pattern, were disappointed and they wouldn't even look at them. So that was my starting point: to create garments with no patterning whatsoever, concen-

Drawings by Gladys Perint Palmer for the Missoni collections

trating instead on the weave and the quality of the materials. Using the factory machinery, I wanted to produce something completely different. It was only a few years ago that I realized the level of professionalism that I had attained through watching my assistants. I had let them help me, allowing them to contribute directly to the company's success, which meant that I was capable of doing this job.'

Tai and Rosita remain the points of reference. Their passion for the applied arts, which goes beyond art for art's sake, has been passed on in its imaginative and creative entirety to their children, now enthusiastic accomplices in an unrivalled project, in a way of working that bears no resemblance whatsoever to the traditional manufacture of yarns and knitwear.

In the Sumirago factory, a stone's throw from home, the prevailing atmosphere is one of an art studio. It is among pieces of knitting, brushstrokes of colour, fragments of material and a love of nature that the initial ideas take shape, prior to being

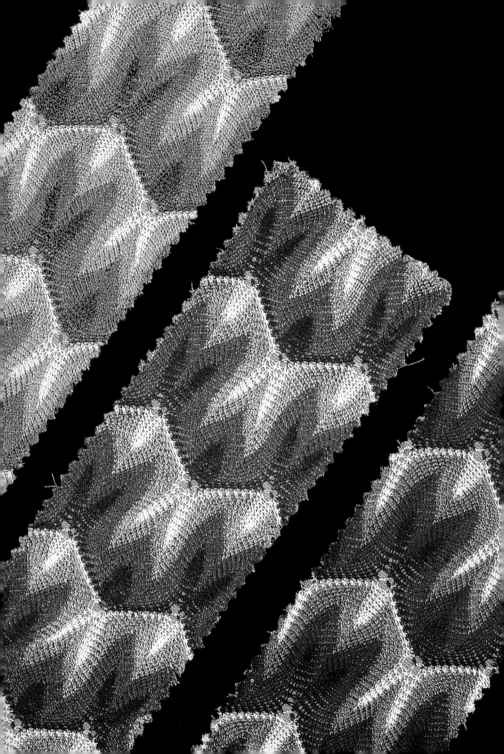

developed on the machines. Luca, entirely in tune with Ottavio's world, transforms these machines into impeccable executors of an abstract, informal, multi-coloured, changeable and inexhaustibly inspired dream. And so today the dreams of father and son have become entwined.

Designed by the architect Enrico Buzzi and inaugurated in 1969, the Sumirago factory is situated in a hilly area, amid woods and fields, with a view over Monte Rosa. Rosita, who grew up in Golasecca, feels passionately about this view which, as Tai has pointed out, enables them 'to work in a place more suited to spending weekends'. Time has reaffirmed this choice of location. It was in this area that first their children, Vittorio, Angela and Luca, and later their grandchildren grew up. While it is natural to plan life around both the home and the business, Tai and Rosita's choices have been inherited by their children who, after playing with wools and fabrics, have developed a relationship of affinity and professional collaboration with their parents.

Art, fashion, materials and ideas take form in a healthy team spirit, in a working environment which, thanks to Tai and Rosita, has never aspired to assume gigantic proportions; on the contrary, they remain faithful to a plan that aims not to compromise either the contribution of each individual, the human dimension, or the active collaboration between the different areas of the company. Increasingly sophisticated, the machines have optimized the rhythms of a refined and complicated production process. Yet the vital importance of creativity in the design and development of images and imagery, entirely unique in quality, has not been forgotten. And so, almost by magic, inimitable and varied results are always achieved. In the course of time, these have been inspired by the colours of the woods surrounding the factory and through the observation of the stars and skies, themes close to Luca's heart. There has never been a lack of influences reflecting an interest in art, in remote cultures, in different attitudes to colour absorbed during travels around the world and related to symbologies, to rituals and to continuously fresh and enlightened interpretations.

Preceding pages:
Left, colour variations of the yarn used in the dress on the right; right, American-style summer knitted dress (photograph by G. Luchford)

Reels of yarn in position and ready for use on the loom

A ccording to the Missoni philosophy, the new signifies venturing into the unknown, reinventing oneself, having total freedom to grow and to change. The fashion critic Anna Piaggi has aptly captured the spirit of this task, 'To me, every collection has been an open book, related to spontaneous reactions, discoveries and journeys, to technical inventions and to preferences of the moment, always guided by the winds of fashion. Was Rosita thinking of Vionnet? Well, look at the cut of the 1991 Spring/Summer collection. What about Tai's interpretation of Africa for Italia '90? Well, a new chromatic and dimensional range appeared in his beloved zigzags. In each collection, in each garment, there have always been stories, a chorus of voices, just like some special fairy-tale. And a contribution from the whole working team. Deciding on a colour? A heated brainstorming session. Describing a wool? A visual and sensual, technical and imaginative experience; particularly when translated into words by Luca Missoni, a true conceptual genius in the Missoni world.' Piaggi continues, 'To cover one's body with the sand of the Sahara, with the frosting flowers of a Viennese cake, with Persian miniatures, with playing cards, or with mosaics from Ravenna, the tiles of San Marco, with butterflies, postcards, wristwatches, Victorian toys? The visual character of fashion by Missoni – symbols, colours, materials, forms – such an integral part of a unique style, has represented one of the most meaningful stimuli during the course of my career as a writer.'

With its highly evocative and yet simultaneously abstract quality, with its careful attention to line and form, at once both soft and informal, and with its capacity to render the female anatomy so totally feminine but also to redefine items in the male wardrobe, Missoni style never contradicts its essential, multi-faceted modernity. Although the womenswear collection has always been distinct from the men's, the Missonis work on a universal idea of clothing, suggesting that a couple can have a single wardrobe, with no dividing lines, which is full of ideas, of possible combinations both for him and for her.

Lightweight knitted garments. Milan collections (photograph by A. Schepis)

This is how Missoni style lends itself so perfectly to a harmonious visual union of feminine and masculine symbols. Forms freed from conventional frameworks; the playful matching of different patterns; stripes and space-dyeing; geometric shapes and landscapes; flowers and tartans all appear in both wardrobes. And although chronologically Missoni gave birth to women's fashion before men's, Anna Piaggi maintains that it was created 'from the rib of Adam (Tai)'. She observes, 'Right from the beginning, the Basic Motivation, particularly in the field of knitwear, has been to define the relationship between form and function, keeping them magically balanced at the cutting edge of fashion. I think, for example, of the confidence, of the ease with which the cardigan has been reinvented, collection after collection…. To transform into a fashion garment an item of knitwear already so rich in connotation called for the solution of so many problems, an infinite amount of technical invention and effects of cut and form which until then had been possible only with fabrics.' Moreover, their aesthetic theorization of the 'put together', launched in 1970, established a new way of looking at how to dress women, and also men, which became increasingly sophisticated and interesting as the years went by, earning them prestigious awards and enthusiastic reviews from the press. In 1983, writing in the *Corriere della Sera*, the celebrated journalist Enzo Biagi commented, 'Ottavio is always on the move, he's playing a very long game, part of an endless gamble. Two scraps of material in every colour, felt-tip pens and squared paper, like kids use at school, are all he needs to express his ideas; and from all this, Rosita will come up with garments that are unmistakable in style.'

While it is only natural that the men's and women's clothing should continuously revolve around the same range of garments, from skirts to trousers, from jackets to waistcoats, from T-shirts to cardigans, from sarongs to shorts, it remains to be understood how Tai's studies of formal and chromatic combinations, coupled with the creativity adopted in cut and form by Rosita, have transformed this union into an inexhaustible source of sensations, discoveries and miracles. Back in 1969, standing before a Missoni collection, Diana Vreeland uttered the memorable phrase, 'Look! Who says that there are only colours? There are also shades!'

*Satin-effect
knitted woman's
suit with bouclé
jacket. Milan
collections
(photograph by
A. Schepis)*

Man's tweed suit with co-ordinated wave-patterned knitted sweater. Milan collections (photograph by A. Schepis)

Man's 'cosmically inspired'
phosphorescent-effect sweater.
Milan collections
(photograph by A. Schepis)

A pattern of stitches in autumn
hues producing a patchwork
effect. Milan collections
(photograph by A. Schepis)

What is considered to be Angela or Luca Missoni's most singular contribution to the family's creative heritage today?

Undoubtedly the answer lies in their ability to render the exception the norm and to present the Missoni image to a new generation of consumers, the ability to bring to instant fruition the accumulation of years of research and experiment carried out by the Tai—Rosita partnership. They have inherited a wealthy patrimony of ideas to be manipulated, to be recombined in a playful and kaleidoscopic manner and to be reinvented on the basis of a changing sensitivity to fashion.

As we head towards the millennium, the Missoni identity is a winning combination of technology and good taste, of subtle and precious layers of fantasy, treated from time to time in a monothematic way. Space-dyeing and zigzags are often protagonists; designs sparkle with lurex; mixed motifs are created by sewing together strips of frayed wool and zigzag-patterned jersey. Or else, as in the latest Autumn/Winter collection, we find embroidery on top of space-dyeing and extremely feminine cuts on minidresses which contrast the electric tones of orange or neon green with black and beige. Pattern on top of pattern is also a predominant characteristic of the men's wardrobe, a palette with which to portray one's own moods and personality.

The door leading to Missoni clothes becoming a versatile and integral part of any modern-day wardrobe has been reopened. With Missoni, the total look is not important and the individual items, mixable and matchable, once again become elements to play with, symbols of style, bearing no similarity whatsoever to anything else on the market. Missoni is Missoni. It is beyond classification, like a language with completely autonomous rules of grammar and syntax, a kind of alien creature that has landed happily on the planet of fashion.

Man and woman's lightweight knitted beachwear. Milan collections (photographs by A. Schepis)

39

Man's lightweight suit with knitted shirt and tie. Milan collections (photograph by A. Schepis)

Woman's winter separates inspired by earth colours and with enamelled belt. Milan collections (photograph by A. Schepis)

Today, examining the minute, exquisite dresses and little sweaters designed by Angela Missoni or looking at the versatility of the shawl-sarongs, capable of taking on at least ten different identities thanks to an ingenious fusion of patterns and freely combined colours, we feel that we have rediscovered the thread of an inexhaustible dialogue. We experience not only the thrill of a style that is timeless, yet modern and inextricably linked to the present, but also the certainty of continuously developing research.

The incessant need for change leads to variations in the consumer's taste and attitudes. The visual identity of each season must therefore reflect these fluctuations in the market.

During the years in which Japanese-style minimalism prevailed, Tai and Rosita established a solid and prestigious position for themselves. It seemed that a new chapter was beginning, one in which innovative instinct was to make its mark in the hallowed realm of the 'classic'. In this apparently stable field of fashion, any radical changes in trends were certainly not foreseen. However, with the seventies revival (the decade which had witnessed the precipitous rise to success of the Missoni look) on the one hand and the energy, enthusiasm, curiosity and willingness to take risks on the other, the Missoni image returned once again to the crest of the wave.

The Missonis are now a recurrent theme on the front covers of the specialist magazines and highly praised by the critics, providing a gentle reflection of fashion's latest developments on the catwalks. The Missonis' vision seems to have entered into a new, close harmony with our own fresh demands.

Around 1996, what Isa Tutino Vercelloni has described as 'a fortunate combination of events' occurred; the space-dyed and zigzag motifs returned to the limelight, while Missoni relaunched them with great creative and imaginative energy. From *Elle France* to American *Vogue*, from the *Herald Tribune* to *Women's Wear Daily*, from costumes created for the opera to those for modern ballet, and from clothing to carpets, glass, jewelry, exhibitions and numerous awards, the Missoni excursus was the fruit of a complementarity of tastes, cultures and emotions, of tirelessly revisiting the best ideas that stem from the very origins of fashion: from Vionnet to Schiaparelli, from Sonia Delaunay to Coco Chanel.

This success reflects a love for an active, contemporary, dynamic and relaxed lifestyle, while paying homage to ethnic iconographies and to the history of costume and

*Unusual knitted bikini and beach
sandals. Milan collections
(photograph by A. Schepis)*

elasticated jersey briefs; right, the opposite combination. Milan collections (photographs by A. Schepis)

couture. The singularity of this investigation led to their work appearing in the Guggenheim Museum in New York. The critic Germano Celant, an affirmed supporter of the transversal relationships linking art, fashion, architecture, photography, design and other forms of visual expression, conceived the exhibition entitled 'The Italian Metamorphosis 1943–1968'. In a highly selective survey and the first examination at an international level of the influence of Italian culture throughout the world, the Missonis found themselves on the extremely exclusive list of those participating in the show.

Tai and Rosita are considered unequivocal leaders in the world-wide phenomenon of 'made in Italy', alongside personalities such as Fontana, Melotti, Giacomelli, Capucci, Valentino, Castiglioni, Burri, Gregotti and other ingenious innovators of the post-war period.

In 1995, this exhibition was followed by the show entitled 'Ottavio e Rosita Story', held in the Galleria Civica d'Arte Moderna in Gallarate and put together by Angelo Jelmini and Luca Missoni. A biographical survey was also drawn up on this occasion and published by Skira. Through the use of elegant graphics and a wealth of colours, motifs, dates and facts, it provided a summary of the Missonis' cultural world. From fashion photographs to the covers of specialist magazines, from their passion for art to that for the history of fashion and from the repertoire of collections and designs emerges the variety and uniqueness of a style that has characterized and continues to single out this couple as one of the most avant-garde and long-sighted phenomena in the field of modern taste. A great source of inspiration both for illustrators, such as Antonio Lopez and Gladys Perint Palmer, and for celebrated journalists and talent scouts, among them Anna Piaggi, Diana Vreeland or Suzy Menkes, Missoni fashion has also inspired photographers such as Steven Meisel, Jean-Baptiste Mondino and Hans Feurer and has aroused the interest of many magazines, including *Vogue Italia*, American *Vogue*, *Women's Wear Daily* and the *Herald Tribune*.

The creative path along which Tai and Rosita have travelled during years of hard work provides the basis for the company's inimitable identity. Missoni's much-emulated and internationally recognized style has earnt it a major place in the history of fashion.

Winter evening dress in lurex wool. Milan collections (photograph by A. Schepis)

*look', inspired by
tales of mermaids.
Milan collections
(photographs by
A. Schepis)*

Long space-dyed scarf

telling image from the fifties, published in the 'Ottavio e Rosita Story' catalogue, shows a knitted lamé suit with a little shoulder-bag in the same material. This was one of the first designs on which the Missoni label appeared and can be seen as a sort of precursor. It anticipates the importance that was to be assumed by detail (from buttons to buckles), by accessories (from handbags to suitcases, umbrellas to tights, hats to scarves, shoes to jewelry) and by the creation of items outside the confines of fashion (designs for plates, vases, cups, rugs, upholstery for sofas and armchairs), reflecting the Missonis' insatiable curiosity to experiment with different materials – a particular characteristic of their collections.

The distinct mark each of the Missonis makes in creating accessories reveals their different cultural interests and passions for colours and materials, but also shows a shared awareness of the spirit of the times and of developments in industrial design and architecture. They demonstrate a knowledge of and passion for modern and contemporary art, making clear references to ethnic cultures, to Africa and to the Orient.

Referring to Rosita's necklaces, Anna Piaggi draws parallels with the art of Oskar Schlemmer, 'The Missonis have even used knitting to produce jewelry, pieces which look as if they come from the Bauhaus *Triadische Ballet!*'. Rosita, on the other hand, confesses that the primary motivation behind her way of working derives from the character of her husband Ottavio, who taught her 'with his contemplative outlook, what he refers to as a philosophy. That is to say, to tackle work in an unrestricted manner, without being bound by pre-established techniques.'

The Missonis' ornament and detail have the plastic potency of works of art. We detect Rosita's touch in subtle, sophisticated and exquisitely impalpable overtones, while Tai's highly spectacular flair emerges in bold and playful stitches and colours.

Forerunners of the universally acclaimed 'made in Italy', the Missonis have mapped out an entire world, complete with wardrobe, furnishings, décor and formal innovations that have taught us to make free associations between past and present, to appreciate and reinvent the culture of our own century.

Preceding pages:
Left, man's suit with
matching knitted and lined
sack-bag; right, T-shirt,
briefs for outdoor wear
and patchwork-effect bag
with stiff lining. Milan
collections (photographs by
A. Schepis)

*Elasticated tights and
wedge-heeled shoes
covered in knitted
material*

In 1971, almost thirty years after that first lamé suit, when the Missonis exhibited their 'patchworks' in Cortina, the press compared these to works in a museum. A further flattering observation was made by Bernardine Morris of the *New York Times*, 'It's what Chanel would be doing if she were still alive, young and working in knits'. In 1991, Ottavio's tapestries were shown for the first time in Japan, at the Yurakucho Asahi Gallery in Tokyo, in an original display organized by Luca Missoni.

The Missonis' ideas subsequently materialized as perfume, as upholstery for Fiat cars and as unmistakable contributions to the world of interior design and household linen. As Pia Soli pointed out in 1976, in the Roman newspaper *Il Tempo*, 'The Missonis represent a new way of living in which luxury has nothing to do with cost; it means genius, imagination, simplicity. The Missonis provide people with clothing for real life, the structures are elementary; and the pieces are full of designs and colours which stand out more strongly with each new season.' The influence of the Missoni accessory alone could nowadays fill an entire retrospective. Way back in the early seventies, they were among the first to create their own distinctive stylistic details, to be found in woollen tights, bathing costumes, gloves, hats, umbrellas and glasses. The Missonis offered dedicated followers of fashion a dual lesson in style: the opportunity to create, layer upon layer, an individual version of the overall Missoni look and also the chance to graft tiny, minute touches of Missoni onto a whole in which the ideas of other designers, items in fabric and monochrome backgrounds could all exist.

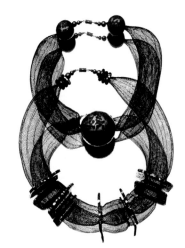

Left, crinoline necklaces; right, interwoven leather bag (photographs by G. Mocafico)

The Missonis have succeeded in conveying to the general public an interest in the applied arts, something which, prior to them, seemed to belong more to the realm of the technical than the practical, more to the traditions of the twentieth century than to the latest in style.

Plexiglass necklace
(photograph by G. Mocafico)

The Missonis' presence at the first Florence Art-Fashion Biennale was, of course, a foregone conclusion. Theirs, perhaps, is one of the labels most frequently associated with a concept of art which has been compared simultaneously to Russian avant-garde painting, to the traditions of abstract and informal art, to experiences employing the environment in art and, lastly, to the capacity to reinvent the very concept of applied art. An article written about them in the catalogue *Looking at Fashion* points out that when a business bears a family's name, it becomes more than just a business, it becomes a heritage. The Missoni heritage is synonymous with family commitment, dedicated hard work and pride in having created an original product. After forty years in the fashion world, Missoni has come to symbolize the essence of the materials themselves, the art of colour and high-quality knitwear.

Luca Missoni, responsible for designing displays and exhibitions of the family's history and ideas, has become the interpreter and director of a sensitivity that has been passed down from generation to generation. He has observed Tai's creative instinct and subsequently made it tangible by creating monumental displays of colour produced with fabric patterns, the play of light and even floral designs, vast tapestries which vividly evoke the idea of oriental mandalas.

Drawings by Antonio Lopez
for the Missoni collections

Drawings by
Antonio Lopez for
the Missoni collections

*Drawings by Gladys
Perint Palmer for the
Missoni collections*

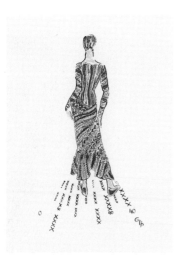

Left, knitted totem poles
at the first Florence Art-
Fashion Biennale; right,
samples of the material
used to create them

Attraverso un bosco
di righe

The family grew up with the responsibility of exporting its own creative vision throughout the world, surrounding itself with various collections, ranging from Sonia Delaunay's drawings to the prototype garments of the Futurist artist Giacomo Balla, from Indian boxes in multi-coloured straw to old stained glass with its amazing array of colours.

With time, this cultural wealth has merged with Luca's love of high technology, of the light of the stars and of the colours of artificial lighting, enabling the Missonis to reconcile the world of fashion with a feeling for art, presenting us with imaginative symbolic interpretations, tangible elaborations of their sense of colour and form.

In 1978, two important monographic exhibitions were held as a celebration of twenty-five years in business: one in the Rotonda della Besana in Milan and the other at the Whitney Museum of American Art in New York.

Since then, the name Missoni has no longer stood simply for fashion, but rather for the phenomenon of the original and fruitful union of fashion, art and design. Even today, when referring to the Missonis, Suzy Menkes writes in terms of 'Italian fashion created from technology and art', a view which Luca endorses, adding, 'Living in a world in which every kind of artistic resource is available, it becomes natural to apply them in a variety of ways.... This leads to a continual pursuit of information.... There are hundreds of paths to explore.'

Their story emerges as one of cultural inquiry, from which nothing is excluded *a priori*. Tireless masters of experiment and great perfectionists, they have succeeded in building their own independent world of ideas and proposals to support the prolific dialogue of their highly successful family coalition.

This dialogue, seen as a cultural phenomenon, one of style and fashion, is attracting a continuously growing swarm of new followers – from the world of cinema to the world of pop, from Jack Nicholson to Alanis Morisette, from Woody Harrelson to Noah. Missoni is hitting the headlines, dressing the young trendsetters in art, cinema and show business, and appearing on the front covers of the most celebrated international magazines. Might this not just mean that the new-found *joie de vivre*, so perfectly expressed by the Missoni world, is all that is required to maintain a position of indisputable importance in the realm of our passions and desires?

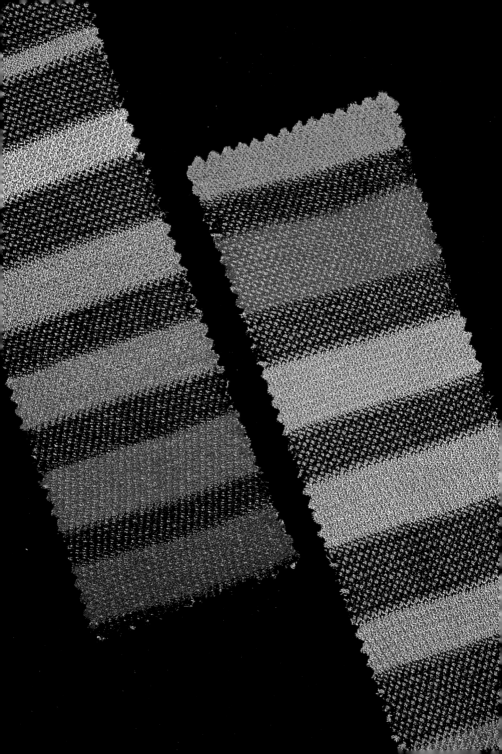

For many years, the celebrated fashion photographer Mario Testino has been associated with the Missonis. His is the mind behind the publicity campaigns and he dictates the way in which the Missoni image is portrayed world-wide. Here, he gives a personal account of his professional career with the Missonis.

How did you start to work with the Missonis?

Before they got in touch with me, they still had some doubts, basically because I was already working on other fashion campaigns. As for myself, looking at their previous campaigns, I had often thought, 'It's incredible how many companies let their image lose impact.' I could sense their desire to make a comeback, but a comeback is difficult…. You can't simply hit on the right image; you also need to use the clothes in a certain way.

What do you think of Missoni fashion?

I have loved it since the seventies. I bought their clothing when I was younger too. I like colour a lot and think that my fondness for Missoni derives mainly from this.

You are perhaps the first photographer who has proved capable of presenting Missoni fashion not simply in terms of clothes, but as a lifestyle. As a world in itself. Your relationship with colour manages to create an atmosphere that reflects them profoundly.

As a fashion photographer you always have to know who you are working with and how to convey their ideas and aspirations. A photographer merely produces, for the general public, the image the stylist has requested. In my profession, you don't create, you interpret. During the first season that I did for them, some of the images that I took with backlight were inspired by the past, by the taste of photographers like Hans Feurer. It was an idea that arose from my associating Missoni with the desert. To me it seemed that the collection had that kind of atmosphere, derived from that particular kind of light. I subsequently went on to conceive and organize the 1997 Spring/Summer campaign for their men and women's collections, which I personally consider to be the most successful to date.

*Bouclé-effect sweater
(photograph by M. Testino)*

I agree with you. It really has incredible atmospheric impact....

It's about colour, but it also manages to convey a certain intellectual aura and at its very heart it deeply reflects their way of being and of relating to fashion.

The casting is also about absolutely perfect faces. These images are true portraits.

I believe in taking great care not to use the same faces for different campaigns. Perhaps because of this, my clients always end up by having complete faith in me.

What kind of relationship have you had with the Missoni family? With whom in particular and on what terms?

Basically, my relationship is with Angela. In a working relationship, I always try to get to know the real person and create a rapport that is direct and upfront. After a fashion show, I take the trouble to go backstage and, instead of saying 'Wonderful! Wonderful!', I might actually offer some criticism, 'The light wasn't quite right, because the clothes look better from the back than the front.' And they or the models will also ask me, 'How did that round go? How are the hands?' and things like that. I think it's totally meaningless not to tell the truth. So, that is the kind of relationship I have had with Angela right from the start. And perhaps I can also understand that she is in a difficult position. Because although they are all members of the same family, they all have their own opinions about things. Angela, however, is a person who is very suited to this set-up. She is open-minded, she accepts advice. It's true, they are the Missonis. But there is no harm in listening to the opinions and views of the people working in close proximity to you.

As a photographer, what is your relationship with the Missonis?

Many people go into this profession because of their love of photography. Others do it because they love the girls. And some, although fewer, because they love fashion. And this is definitely my case. As far as I'm concerned, it is not difficult to grasp that Gucci and Missoni have completely different needs when promoting their image. Consequently, in clearly divergent situations I manage to sense what is the right thing to do. Going back to the Missonis, I have to say that they are incredibly warm, generous people who are not afraid of showing their feelings.

Knitted suit with gaucho-style skirt (photograph by M. Testino)

I sensed this when Rosita first came up to me and

Different ideas for men's knitwear
to be worn under jackets
(photographs by M. Testino)

said, 'Well done, Mario!'. I think that their greatest achievement in the Autumn/Winter 1998 collection lies in having transformed Missoni into a style for the city. The choice of multi-coloured necklaces, with no ethnic overtones or emphasis on luxury, has underlined the versatility of a contemporary wardrobe, suited to everyday life, from work to the smartest occasions. In other words, you no longer have to imagine you're in the mountains to wear these clothes!

I think this openness is part of Missoni's recent success.

Knitwear is an attitude. It's quite natural that it should make you feel different from when you're wearing a suit in fabric. It gives you freedom of movement, but this doesn't necessarily mean it can only be worn outdoors or for practising sport.

What has changed in your professionalism today?

There was a long period in which no one offered me any work. I have probably grown more mature, I have more confidence in my decisions. At the beginning, I worked with Franca Sozzani while she was at *Lei* and *Per Lui*. Then one day she said to me, 'I'm going to work for *Vogue* and you're coming with me.' It was probably no bad thing that I answered back when she bossed me about, saying, 'Do this, do that.' I replied, 'I want to do as I please. If I don't follow my own path and instead do things to please you, tomorrow I will no longer be what I feel I ought to be. So, I am not working until I can do whatever I feel like doing.' Having said that, she was the one who gave me the chance to do what I wanted. And, nowadays, I can honestly say that I learnt everything from Franca. She once said to me, 'Here are the clothes, here's the money, do what you like.' You know, when someone gives you that much freedom, it is impossible not to feel grateful.

A final word on the future of Missoni.

I think they'll go far. Because they give space to the people around them. And, season after season, this increases the feeling of truth, of authenticity, that you sense in their collections. They are collections that are real, like the people who created them. For this reason, with every season, they'll go further. It is an ongoing process, the tangible proof of a certain, special loyalty to themselves.

Knitted maxidress
(photograph by M. Testino)

Left, American-style knitted dress with zigzag patterns; right, tweed-effect knitted poncho (photographs by M. Testino)

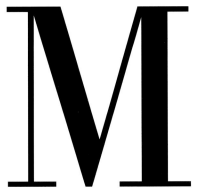

Missoni style is not only for top models, but also for show-business personalities, as an expression of elegance and glamour. In fact, the actress Halle Berry, judged by the American magazine *In Style* to be one of the world's most elegant women, wore Missoni to collect her Golden Globe award. The sweet-faced and beautiful Nastassia Kinski, daughter of the actor Klaus, also chose to wear a mermaid-style dress designed by Missoni.

The celebrated 'coloured yarns' are also much loved by highly individual men, such as the actor Woody Harrelson (star of the film *Larry Flint*), who appears very relaxed in a brightly coloured knitted shirt by Missoni. Most surprising of all, perhaps, is the boxer Jack Johnson who, despite belonging to the most macho of worlds, has also opted for the softness of wool and the harmony of Missoni colours.

Mermaid-style dress worn by the top model Eva Herzigova (photograph by G. Barbieri)

Woody Harrelson and Halle
Berry wear Missoni

Nastassia Kinski and the boxing champion Jack Johnson wear Missoni

Franca Sozzani

The Missonis' skill derives from the way they never recycle ideas.

Vogue Italia

They have carefully managed to avoid every kind of revival or reworking of their past. For this reason, their collections always seem totally contemporary.

*Tunic dress with zigzag patterns
(photograph by M. Testino)*

Seventies-inspired zigzag suit
(photograph by R. Camerun)

Diana
Vreeland

American *Vogue*

Look!
Who says that there
are only colours?
There are also
shades!

Man's knitted co-ordinates
(photograph by M. Testino)

The cover of Vogue Italia *no. 545*
(photograph by S. Meisel)

Aldo Premoli

Uomo Vogue

Ottavio and Rosita Missoni are two genuine and extremely refined people who, throughout their entire career, have managed to steer well clear of commonplaces in fashion. Today, I believe these characteristics to be at the very foundation of their renewed success. Surrounded by young people and in accordance with their creative integrity, Ottavio and Rosita have therefore widened and expanded their own production and invention opportunities. Never becoming authoritarian or egocentric, they have granted the new recruits freedom to act. And this attitude has produced, as we can see, excellent results!

*Terry-knit jacket
(photograph by M. Testino)*

*Mermaid-style dress worn by
the top model Shalom
(photograph by M. Aldridge)*

Following pages:
*Shirt with American-style
neckline and zigzag trousers
(photograph by M. Woolley)*

Gianni Mura

Epoca

Mura dedicates a four-page spread to the Missonis, under the title

Agnelli, Ferrari, Fellini and... the Missoni.

Woman's knitted co-ordinates
(photograph by M. Testino)

Hebe Dorsey

International Herald Tribune

The Missonis are doing something that only great designers can do. They have established a style which they keep improving upon, rather than making rash changes every season.

Woman's co-ordinates
consisting of layers of
space-dyed garments
(photograph by M. Testino)

Bill Cunningham

Chicago Tribune

Sensational knitwear in Italy. Colours that are a revelation of nature's beauty… in an absolutely unexpected mixture, catching the free atmosphere of today's fashion. The buyers from the most important department stores were queuing up in front of the Missonis' apartment in the Plaza Hotel.

*Man's space-dyed sweater
(photograph by M. Testino)*

*Extremely finely knitted shirt
and striped minishorts
(photograph by P. Ogden)*

*Woman's multi-coloured
knitted co-ordinates
(photograph by H. Feurer)*

Centre, man's striped sweater
(photograph by J. Astor)

Above, Paris boutique;
above right and right,
New York boutique

Missoni Boutiques World-wide

Italy
Boutique Missoni Via Sant'Andrea
20121 Milano tel. 0039-2-76003555

Boutique Missoni Piazza di Spagna 78
00187 Roma tel./fax 0039-6-6792555

Boutique Missoni
Calle Valleresso 1312/B
30124 Venezia
tel. 0039-41-5205733
fax 0039-41-5205282

Boutique Missoni Piazzetta dei Pini 95
80077 Ischia Porto (Napoli)
tel. 0039-81-981857
fax 0039-81-997781

Boutique Missoni
Via Vittorio Emanuele 24/B
12051 Alba (Cuneo)
tel./fax 0039-173-34928

Boutique Missoni Piazzetta degli Archi
07020 Porto Cervo (Sassari)
tel. 0039-798-94587

France
Boutique Missoni
436 Rue du Bac 75007 Paris
tel. 0033-1-45483802
fax 0033-1-45484290

Germany
Boutique Missoni
Amiraplatz 3 D - 80333 München
tel. 0049-89-295484
fax 0049-89-229174

Boutique Missoni
Albrecht Dürer Platz 5
D - 90403 Nürnberg
tel. 0049-911-2449419
fax 0049-911-2449409

Boutique Missoni Meinekestrasse 5
D - 10719 Berlin
tel./fax 0049-30-883127

United States
Boutique Missoni 836 Madison Avenue
New York, NY 10021

tel. 001-212-5179339
fax 001-212-4396037

Japan
Boutique Missoni Sonnette Aoyama
4-21-26 Minami Aoyama Minato-Ku
Tokyo 107
tel. 0081-3-34239433

Boutique Missoni Osaka Gallery H
1-6-20 Higashi Shinsaibashi Chuo-Ku
Osaka-Shi, Osaka 542
tel. 0081-6-2531471

Boutique Missoni
Nagoya Hilton Plaza 1-3-3 Sakae
Naka-Ku Nagoya Shi, Aichi 460
tel. 0081-6-25314955
fax 0081-522121440

Taiwan
Boutique Missoni 320, Sec 1
Tun Hwa S. Road Taipei
tel. 00886-2-3755278
fax 00886-2-3759930

Boutique Missoni Regent Hotel
B1 n. 3 Lane 39
Sec 2 Chung Shan N. Road
Taipei
tel. 00886-2-5118352

Hong Kong
Boutique Missoni
3501 Gloucester Tower
The Landmark, Central Hong Kong
tel. 00852-28770211

Singapore
Boutique Missoni/Libesa 1,
Claymore Drive
18-04 Orchard Towers
Singapore 0923
tel. 0065-7327859
fax 0065-7344620

Korea
Boutique Missoni
99-17 Cheongdamdong
Kang Nam Ku, Seoul
tel. 0082-2-54812460
fax 0082-2-5156932

Chronology

1921

Ottavio Missoni, known as Tai, is born in Ragusa (Dalmatia) to Teresa de Vidovich, Countess of Capocesto and Ragosniza, and to the sea captain Vittorio, son of a Friuli magistrate who had moved to Dalmatia while it was still Austrian territory.

During his childhood, the family moves to Zara. Tai studies first in Trieste and then in Milan.

1931

Rosita Jelmini is born in Golasecca, a village on the banks of the Ticino, in the province of Varese. Not far from her home is the factory founded by the Torrianis, her maternal grandparents, producing shawls and embroidered fabrics, where her parents Angelo Jelmini and Diamante Torriani work.

Ottavio returns to Italy at the end of the year, living partly in Trieste and partly in Milan.

1947

Ottavio starts up a knitwear business in Trieste with his friend Giorgio Oberwerger. In a small factory, equipped with only four machines, he produces woollen 'Venjulia' track suits. These were adopted as the uniform for the Italian team at the 1948 Olympic Games.

1949

Having completed her studies, Rosita begins to take part in the creative side of the family business, following in the footsteps of her father, Angelo Jelmini.

1953

On 18 April, Ottavio and Rosita marry in Golasecca, moving to 12, Via Vespucci, Gallarate. They set up a small knitting workshop in the basement and work together on the business that Ottavio started in Trieste.

1954

Vittorio is born on 25 April.

1955

Ottavio and Rosita work for the Biki boutique in Milan, together with Louis Hidalgo, with whom they were later to design small, exclusive collections for the Rinascente department store in Milan.

1956
Luca is born on 4 July.

1958
The small fashion collection christened 'Milano-Simpathy' is presented at La Rinascente. A shirt-dress with brightly coloured stripes dominates the window display in the Piazza del Duomo. Brunetta captures it, in characteristically rapid and immediate style, for a full-page advertisement in the *Corriere della Sera*. The Missoni label had recently been sewn on these clothes. Angela is born on 26 December.

1960
Missoni clothes start to feature in fashion magazines.

1961
As business expands, they move the workshop to 16, Via Cattaneo, Gallarate.

1962
Rediscovery of the Rachel knitting machine, which until then had been used solely for making shawls. They use it to create innovative, brightly coloured and extremely lightweight garments.

1963
They start to experiment with rayon, which later becomes one of their favourite fibres. Leaving a successful career in banking, Umberto Monte joins the venture and takes on the task of managing the business.

1965
With the infallible instinct of a talent scout, Anna Piaggi becomes the first journalist to take a serious interest in Tai and Rosita's work. Fashion editor for *Arianna* (a Mondadori publication), Piaggi, together with her husband, the photographer Alfa Castaldi, continues to follow them step by step, season after season, publicizing their collections through highly individual 'releases' and the coining of phrases that have gone down in history, such as the ingenious 'identiknit'.

Rosita's parents invite her to go on the liner *Michelangelo*'s maiden voyage from Genoa to New York. Through common friends, whom Rosita had met on her frequent business trips to Paris, she meets the young French designer Emmanuelle Kahn in New York and proposes working together.

1966
Their first fashion show, held at the Gerolamo theatre in Milan, is enthusiastically received by the press. The collection marks a break from traditional views of uses for knitwear.

1967
In April, for the first time, they take part in the fashion shows held at the Pitti Palace in Florence. They make their first appearance on the front cover of *Arianna*.

At the last minute, Rosita realizes that the models are not wearing what Marilyn Monroe referred to as 'intimacies' of the right colour for their thin lamé blouses and sends them down the catwalk with nothing underneath. Under the bright lights, the tops become transparent, resulting in a flood of protest from the establishment, 'Where do they think they are, Crazy Horse?'. Elsa Rossetti heads her article, 'A sexy evening at Florence fashion showings', commenting, 'The ideas of Missoni were the most freakish and eccentric of the day'. Not everyone appreciated it, however, and so, the following season, while the nude look was being launched in Paris by Yves Saint Laurent, Tai and Rosita were not invited to show in Florence. They therefore took the opportunity to show their summer collection in Milan, at the Solari swimming pool, in what was described as 'a singular and memorable aquatic fashion show' featuring inflatable chairs and floating, transparent furniture.

1968

A Missoni design is featured on the cover of *Elle*. They receive the Moda Mare award for beachwear in Cefalù.

1969

In April, *Women's Wear Daily*, the paper considered by many to be the fashion Bible, devotes its opening page to the Missonis, commenting, 'Missoni is in the lead, with one of the most sinful dresses among those inspired by Art Deco'.

Through Consuelo Crespi, Tai and Rosita meet Diana Vreeland at the Grand Hotel in Rome. 'Look! Who says that there are only colours? There are also shades!' was Vreeland's famous comment on this occasion. A fairy godmother and tutelary deity from across the ocean, she immediately sets up a series of meetings for them in the United States with leading buyers.

The new factory at Sumirago is built, to a design by Enrico Buzzi.

1970

Marvin Traub, president of Bloomingdale's, decides to open a Missoni boutique, the first in the United States, within the prestigious department store. In April, Tai and Rosita once more break new ground and present a highly successful collection in Florence, launching a new and striking way of dressing both women and men. The style the Americans were to christen 'put together' is born. Ottavio and Rosita Missoni become 'i Missoni'.

1971

In Cortina, the Missonis show a collection featuring the celebrated 'patchworks', employing them in an entirely new way. The press start to compare Ottavio's colour compositions to works of contemporary art. They receive the Moda Mare award in Capri.

1972

In the spring, the *Los Angeles Times* presents the Missonis as 'The New Status Symbol of Italian Design'. In May, in an article dedicated to the Missonis, Bernardine Morris writes in the *New York Times*, 'They make the best knits in the world, some say the best clothes in the world.' In November, in an editorial entitled 'Who has Fashion Power?', *Women's Wear Daily* ranks the Missonis among the top twenty Fashion Powers in the world.

1973

In November, in Dallas, the Missonis receive the Neiman Marcus Fashion Award. Since it was established in 1938, this prestigious international award, fashion's equivalent to the Oscars, has been presented to names such as Schiaparelli, Chanel, Dior, Pucci and even Georges Braque for his jewelry designs.

From this year onwards, the 'Missoni patchwork' can be seen at the Museum of Modern Art in New York. Other 'Missonis' are exhibited at the Dallas Museum of Art and at the Museum of Costume in Bath, England. The first household linen collection is launched, produced in the United States by Fieldcrest.

1974

The Missonis abandon Florence and the Pitti catwalks. To be able to present their collections in their entirety, they choose Milan, their natural headquarters. The French magazine *Marie Claire* devotes a six-page spread to the collection, under the following title, '*Art: une leçon de tricot et de couleur.... L'inspiration d'un nouveau style.*' Beginning of the partnership with Giorgio Saporiti, with furniture produced by Saporiti Italia upholstered in Missoni fabrics.

1975

A special editorial entitled, 'The best clothes in the world', published in February in American *Vogue* and dedicated to the twenty greatest fashion designers, lists the Missonis among the ten European 'big guns', that is to say, among the designers most influencing the way we dress.

In September, Renato Cardazzo pays homage to Ottavio's work by organizing a one-man show at the Naviglio gallery in Venice, where his fabrics are exhibited as true paintings. Guido Ballo publishes the catalogue *Missoni e la macchina mago* (*Missoni and the Magician-Machine*). Ferruccio Landi writes a comprehensive critique of the show in an article entitled, 'Missoni: a work of art in pullover form'.

1976

The Missoni boutique opens in Milan.

Together with Gianni Agnelli, Prince Charles and Robert Redford, Ottavio is voted one of the world's ten most elegant men.

In the field of household linen, the Missonis are presented the 1976 Tommy Award, the sought-after prize for printed fabrics awarded by the American Printed Fabric Council Inc.

1978

The Missonis summarize the story of their twenty-five-year working career in a spectacular retrospective exhibition organized at the Rotonda della Besana in Milan. The show is a huge success and, in October, travels to the Whitney Museum of American Art in New York, which, for the first time, has agreed to exhibit fashion in its prestigious galleries.

Ottavio exhibits his fabrics at the Torbandena gallery in Trieste.

1980

The perfume 'Missoni' is launched in New York. Beginning of the collaboration with Fiat, studying designs for car interiors. Their boutique in Paris opens.

1982

Their perfume wins the Fragrance Foundation Award for best packaging. Ottavio organizes exhibitions of tapestries in Munich, at the Haus der Kunst, and in Stockholm, at the Blumenthal gallery.

1983

The Missonis make their debut at La Scala in Milan as costume designers for *Lucia di Lammermoor*, directed by Pier Luigi Rizzi and starring Luciano Pavarotti and Luciana Serra, creating over one hundred costumes for the occasion.

Beginning in 1983, Missoni establishes licensing deals with prestigious companies including Marzotto, Safilo and Malerba.

1984

Opening of a new Missoni boutique in Madison Avenue, New York.

1986

The Missonis are awarded the Premio Italia for printed fabrics by the Associazione Serca. They take part in the exhibition 'Futurismo & Futurismi', designing objects and accessories on this theme. The Missonis sponsor 'Comedy Italian Style', a cinema exhibition held at the Museum of Modern Art, New York. On this occasion, they show their collection in the halls of the museum. In June, Rosita is honoured as a Commendatore al merito della Repubblica italiana by the President of the Italian Republic.

1988

In May, Ottavio is awarded the honour of Commendatore al merito della Repubblica italiana by the President of the Italian Republic.

1990

At the seventh Night of Stars gala held in New York, Rosita is presented with the International Prize for Design by Fashion Group International, an organization comprising six hundred American fashion reporters, 'for having influenced, in a decisive manner, the field of fabric and fashion design, creating a style'. On 30 November, again in New York, the Missonis receive a Special Lifetime Achievement Award at the Gala Italia for their great international success in improving the image and status of Italy and of fashion. Rosita is awarded the De Wan Donna di Successo prize.

1991

Ottavio's tapestries are exhibited in Japan for the first time, at the Yurakucho Asahi Gallery in Tokyo.

1992

In February, in Munich, they are presented with the 1992 Mode-Woche Award, a prestigious recognition 'of their contribution to affirming the creativity and capacity for innovation in Italian fashion'. A spectacular fashion show is held at the Prinzregententheater to celebrate the event.

1993

The fortieth anniversary of their marriage and working partnership. On 2 June, Ottavio is awarded the honour of Cavaliere al merito del Lavoro by the President of the Italian Republic.

1994

In March, David Parsons asks the Missonis to design the costumes for the David Parsons Dance Company's latest production, *Step into My Dream*.

During the fashion shows held in July, Pitti Immagine and the city of Florence award Ottavio and Rosita the Premio Pitti Immagine. To mark the occasion, Pitti Immagine organizes the exhibition 'Missonologia', held in the Ridotto of the Pergola theatre in Florence. A catalogue is published bearing the same name. In October, 'Missonologia' is expanded and displayed in the Museo Società per le Belle Arti ed Esposizione Permanente in Milan.

1995

Ottavio and Rosita hold an exhibition in Gallarate, organized by Luca Missoni and Angelo Jelmini. The catalogue is published by Skira.

1996

At the end of 1995 and the beginning of 1996, the Missonis hold an exhibition in two Japanese museums, the Sezon Museum of Art and Nagoya City Museum, again organized by Luca Missoni. The shows are hugely successful, both being visited by more than fifty thousand people.

1997

The Art-Fashion Biennale in Florence, with displays created by Luca Missoni, at the Stazione Leopolda.

Following pages:
Tai and Rosita at the final show
of the Milan collections
(photograph by A. Schepis)

Acknowledgments

The publishers wish to thank the Missoni family, Mariuccia Casadio, Giovanna Sioli, Stefano Peccatori, Stefano Tosi, Caterina Giavotto, Elisa Seghezzi, Mario Testino and Isa Tutino Vercelloni. Thanks are also due to Franca Sozzani (*Vogue Italia*), Aldo Premoli (*Uomo Vogue*), Anna Piaggi, Inter-Events Italia, Arturo Carlo Quintavalle, the Biennale di Firenze and Alessandra Della Porta Rodiani.

Particular thanks go to the Missoni archive for having provided all the images by Miles Aldridge, Joseph Astor, Giampaolo Barbieri, Regan Camerun, Hans Feurer, Glen Luchford, Steven Meisel, Denis Malerbi, Guido Mocafico, Jean-Baptiste Mondino, Perry Ogden, A. Schepis, Mario Testino, Oliviero Toscani and Michael Woolley. Holders of rights to any unidentified photographic material are invited to bring the matter to the attention of the originating publishers, Leonardo Arte.

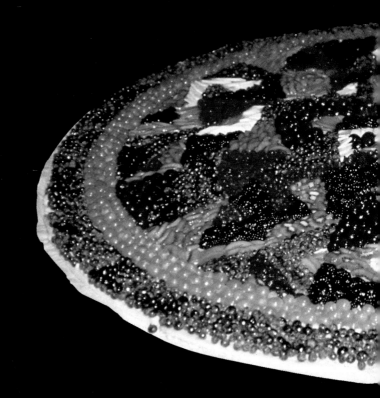

Cake created by Rosita Missoni